Sheltered by Islands

New and Selected Poems

1985-1995

Daniel Thomas Moran

Library of Congress Cataloging In Publication Data

Moran, Daniel Thomas
Sheltered By Islands
I. Title
ISBN-0-9629221-2-9   pbk., $15.00
Jacket designed by Michael Stromberg
Cover Photo William E. Barksdale
Published in The United States of America

For Victoria, Lindsay, Ashley, and Gregory with love

and in memory of my dear friend
William E. Barksdale
1927-1995

Some of the poems in this book were previously published in the following periodicals:

For August Mosca, Another Conspiracy Theory, Never Cross a Woman, *Nassau Review*; After Having Lost It, *Raindog Review*; Pride, The Nature of Worship, Lying with Marianne On St. Mark's Place, *Long Island Quarterly*; Melancholy, With Ignatow At The Whitman Birthplace, *Confrontation*; William Carlos Williams Gets A Haircut, An Ascension, Gestation, *Proteus*; Downbeat, *Sulfur River Literary Review*; Finding Jesus, *New Press Literary Quarterly*; The Saint's Foot, *Nomad's Choir*; The Nature of Forgiveness, *Rocket Literary Quarterly*; Massapequa, *In Autumn, An Anthology of Long Island Poetry*; Omar Geometrics, Valentine's Day 1994, B-Movie, A Trip To The Zoo, *Inky Blue*.

Excerpted from *Dancing for Victoria* (1991) were: The Saint's Foot, The Ballerina At Three, Ashley Zurl, Gregory Riordan, Ode To Molly McConville, Homefires, Shelter Island Presbyterian Sunday, Water, Real Blonde, A Trip To The Zoo, After Keats Ode To A Nightingale.

Exerpted from *Gone to Innisfree* (1993) were: A Man Born of Heroes, Lying With Marianne On St. Mark's Place, A Mother and Son, William Carlos Williams Gets A Haircut, Some Call It Love, Inspiration, God, Harlem Sunday Afternoon, Calverton, Abraham and Son, Massapequa.

In addition, many of these poems contained herein have been broadcast over Long Island Public Radio 88.3 FM WPBX Southampton, New York and on Peconic Bay Television, Riverhead, New York.

Table of Contents

We Mortals
For William E. Barksdale

We long for
the perfection
in these things
of the world;
life, certain
in its
bilateral symmetry;
generations
strung like pearls
on imagined wire.
We squint
at the sun.
We marvel
at the plaintive
syllables of songbirds.
We admire
tallness and clarity.
Feeling the vibrations
of it all beneath our feet,
we rhapsodize
distances
suggested upon
moonless nights,
daring to name
the ineffable.

We write
poems and chant
to the mysteries.
We dance
round fires
in the clearings
we have made
in the forest.
We weep
for the spirits
of fallen trees.
Facing death
we avert our eyes.
When great things
succumb
we tell
ourselves
they were never there.
Thirsty,
we lie
on our backs
allowing our mouths
to fill with rainwater,
and hope to rise
like blossoms
from the dust.

A Man Born of Heroes

My father was a strain-hardened man,
galvanized by years of train tracks
and placards on roadsides which
told him what to dream about.
He believed in many things
which never believed in him,
Bishops and Board Chairmen and
Saints and Coaches and Souls which
played somewhere behind the stars.
He saw a world of square holes
which demanded corners sharp and smooth;
life a closet of gray suits and
black wing-tips, cleaned, pressed
and polished ready for the next day and
the next, hair never beyond the
white collars snug about his neck.
He came home each night, shoulders
stooped, with the island of Manhattan
strapped to his back and left
again each day just as the constellations
were dwindling into the distant sunrise.
He followed his father, who carried
a gold Busman's watch in the fore-pocket
of his threadbare trousers, saved
dimes for Dickens and The National Geographic,
scanned maps for the lands of promise
and captained green buses along avenues
paved with sweat and sorrows,
measuring the moments until his debt
to hardship was paid in full; the
home on the quiet street, the car,
the lawn, the rose-bushes.
And he had followed his father who
was a captain of fine steeds,
banished from the sad Counties of Erin
for loving the jewels of justice by
Victoria's brutal henchmen; tossed
across the cruel shoulders of the
North Atlantic to a brownstone in Harlem

where he hoped his God could recall
mercy and his children could dare to imagine.
And now myself, on another island
beside another sea, pouring out words
Great-grandfather could never fashion,
without god or timepieces, embittered
by our pyrrhic victory, a thrall
to a pen and ever dreaming of
Ireland.

Valentine's Day 1994

I want to sit with
you again,
like we once did
beneath
the easy weight
of new bedding,

In love with you
like a blindman
loves colors,
your gentle head
nested at my shoulder,
your hair a botanica.

We sat in the dark
illuminated by
the grey heartbreak
of Wuthering Heights.
As Merle Oberon died
in Olivier's arms,

I looked at you
and something
in our eyes
said, almost outloud,
I love you
that much.

You To Me

You to me,
are the chapel of all that is true.
The golden stroking smoothstep.
An antidote to the sickness
of miserable existence.
A sip of jasmine tea in a steamy hot tub.
A woolly red sweater on a chilly porch swing.
An electric first kiss rush.
A stapleless gatefold beauty.
The quiet confidence of an old housecat.
The sharpness of newbroken crystal.
A mountain top collecting sun above the mist.
You are the way home.
The flint to a poet's fire.
The sound of crickets in the August hotnight.
A crackling log in a Christmas Eve snow.
The soothing whisper of motherlove.
A goosedown wrap on a winter bed.
A head turner heart burner.
Silk stockings under bluejeans.
The taste of sugar on a child's tongue.
An extra big pieslice.
The words to a sweetsong.
A coolwind kiss on a July highnoon.
Moonlight through bare treetops.
My foreverdream in a jeweled box.

The Ballerina at Three
(for Lindsay Alison)

The ballerina at three
spinning
wild as freedom
elation overwhelming
balance
Nutcracker strains
whirl 'round her
Sugar Plum Fairy
Pizzicato Princess
Arms reach
like spring petals
Eyes lit
with exuberance
The ballerina at three
spins the world
'round, 'round, and
around her.

Ashley Zurl

Do ye know me, Ashley Zurl?
Whose gaze alights my spirit.
Lying adorned in such innocence,
Your radiance bids me near it.

Do ye love me, Ashley girl?
Do your azure eyes behold me?
And though no words adorn your lips,
Such stories you have told me.

Ashley of my love conceived,
I see thee as my mirror.
Hearing the cadence of mine own heart,
And the one heart I hold dearer.

Precious one elate with me,
For the countless meadows yet ahead.
The taste of dew and all things new,
Fields of rosebuds moist and red.

Ashley Zurl, my Ashley girl,
Your life, a treasure I've beholden.
No softer breath could warm my soul,
Nor possession be more golden.

Gregory Riordan

Somewhere
inside these
towers of smokey glass
Among cries of
burgeoning motherhood
Above
the choir of
electric whooshing heartbeats
Down
among the
snag and snarl of wire tubing
Just
after the
deep October night
After
he is certain
the horizon is his alone
Then
the starscape and
the face of Luna
will dim and
a son will rise.

Ode to Molly McConville

Molly McConville died,
After her last noon sun Saturday,

In a lonesome white room,
That was far from her true home.

So very tired and broken,
By eighty-five years of living,

And from hiding so long,
Deep inside of her own thoughts.

Not a soul knew her truly,
This Molly McConville,

Through her days five and fourscore,
Which passed by her so slowly.

And she made life breathe for many,
Including this poor heart,

But never strolled in the garden,
Which she herself planted.

She just shook back her sadrags,
Like a martyr for love lost,

Til she could follow her Teddy
To a place in forever.

Where he waited so saintly,
Nineteen years to the hour,

For the sweet smiling eyes,
Of his Molly McConville.

To August Mosca
New Year's Eve 1994

We sit together, here
in your studio.
Old cedar and evidence
of hardship and joy.
The many canvases
adorn browning walls,
each bearing
one moment defined.
Skylight guides northlight
to floorboards beside
the potblack woodstove
where our boot tips meet.
On your easel
a pastel lady reclines
upon a favored cloth.

You tell me of doubt
and privation,
fruits and conquest,
rain against shingle and
the quiet of light.
Your hands bear secrets
under the subtle strains
of vision and imagination,
dreams realized and
those not yet arrived.
To me, you are
the first star I touch
reaching up into night.
One day it
will be I in your chair,

My hair the color of ashes
my shoulders rounded and heavy,
speaking of truth time taught,
of exhilaration and regret,
recalling all those words
Mosca said.

It's too bad we could not have been
young together, warming ourselves
in the Maytime sun
admiring the soft crescents of
a pastel lady.

The Nature of Poets

I love
sunny days
through
a window
from
a comfortable chair.

When
it
rains
I
go
outside.

Lying With Marianne On St. Marks Place

In the bookshop on St. Mark's Place
I'm lying with Marianne Moore
Spine to spine, beneath
hard covers, shelved neatly
for posterity by the
motherly fingers of
soft friends.
She loves her men
silent and I love
my ladies profound.
There we lie, poised
in our communal in-
spirations, naked
musings and alliteration.
Often in the padlocked
midnight, I wait for
her to turn and embrace
me but still,
she acts as though she
never even knew me.

Another Conspiracy Theory

Everett works
for
Meyer's Parking Garage,
midblock E. 21st.
It says so
on a whitebuttondown
he had been fitted for
at least several years ago.
His green jazzbow
is cocked down
on one side as
though a
tiny man was sitting
on one end,
while he spoke
to Everett.

Everett was
from
Somewhere Uptown
and rode on
tiny elevators only up
and listened all night
to the sound
of dollar bills palming
and radials chirping
on the slick ramps.
"Ya know the Kennedys
and Martin and Malcolm
was all killed by
Buffalo Bob Smith
using Annette Funicello's
mob connections."

Everett threw
back
His Big Shoulders
like a man who
had spent years on
submarines.
"Her Mother's Godmother
was a second cousin
to a Luciano."
He whispered that
to me just
as he had heard it,
from the tiny man
on his tie, certain
I would keep his secret,
at least until I

was back above ground.

Homefires

I'm looking forward
to a place to call home,
with a rack by the door,
to catch my sorry old hat
again, and again.
A familiar aroma
to fill my nostrils.
I'd like a big old chair
to fit my tired self
like a favorite shoe,
near a fire where I can sit,
contemplate my fortunes
and woes,
hold my babes in lap
and tell them
all the tales I've collected
in the days gone before.
And watch snowflakes
land melting like dreams,
on the big shadetree I
had planted with just
a spade and a palm.

First In Love

First in love
with you, I
could spend
hours a day
watching you
dress, bathe,
apply radiance
to your face
with tiny pencils
color and cotton.

So deeply I fell,
plummeting
into the center
of you.

After ten years,
love as deep,
evenings I sprawl
across an old sofa,
with the rented movie
ready to roll
and wonder,
what the hell
could be taking
so long.

A Mother and Son

Through the grasp of
oak branch and glass, the
sweet light of morning reaches
a place beside her where
she lies silent among
the tussled linens.

The tiny boy draws the nectar
from her breast; lips moist petals
gentle as the fingers of the
new day; his eyes closed but
barely, small breaths
stroke her skin.

She is thinking of his
so many somedays, when his arms
will grow strong, his
legs tall.

In my head I hears the notes
of a thousand lullabies and
revel in the ultimate joys
of helplessness.

Bear Facts

Way out there
beyond
The Golden Gates
In
Places where
neighborhoods
meet wilderness
When
Brown Bears
lose their
fear of humans
and come
down from
hilly forests
to dip in pools
and pick
through garbage
Good men
who know best
say
"You can't trust
a friendly bear."
and then they
shoot 'em
deader than
a Sagamore Hill throw-rug.
Dogs, it seems
is just the opposite.

Never Cross a Woman
For Eileen

There she came, as if from
nowhere; Betty Friedan,
the Mother of all wo-
man; The feminine my-
stic lobbying just-
ice with an upraised
fist, high priestess of
uterine actual-
ization. There she came in
a rusty old Ply-
mouth daring as she must to
navigate the tight
spots; careening off of
the nice lady's
new Beemer in the noon-
time bedlam of a Sag
Harbor summer and step-
ped out to the con-
frontation. The lady said,
"Save the speech, Betty. Who's
going to pay for the god-
damned crease in my door? When
my husband sees this, he's going to kill
me."

To Weathermen

You forever
stay put, there
before your
many geographies.
A pig-tail of wire
dives from your ear
into your blazer collar.
How you must suffer,
imprisoned there
in that windowless space,
preaching well
beyond the wee hours
of fronts and gales,
raindrops on floodplains,
groundstrikes and hailstones,
dark followed by

day.

Santa Anna Nor'easter
Bermuda High Heatpump
Waterspouts Snowmakers
The Melting Polar Icecap.
Nine on a scale of ten.
Bonechill and frying eggs
on the sidewalk.
Taking a look from space.
If only
you could step
outside.
Live for
the moments.
Tell us when
it will
all end and

how.

Conclusions Drawn After Passing Yet Another Dead Squirrel In The Street

Frantic

Over

Imminent

Winter

They

Forget

To

Lookboth

Ways.

The Saint's Foot

A day will come when
I will gaze into
These eyes of yours
And they will be deeper even
Than jade in the sea
Framed in soft pine
Living has worn and polished like
A bronze statue of some saint
Whose foot gleams smooth from
The touch of the adoring masses
Who must come to stroke it.

Down Beat

Sun newly down
         standing on hard pavement
in front of the open
             bluedoor of Canio's Books,
     I'm inhaling the
    exhaled smoke of Jack Micheline. Air
is heavy with
            bullshit and vaporous poems
     Tomorrow
        rain for sure.
The combusted tobacco waits
      beside him like
an apparition. I say
    Hey Jack
   and he grabs my hand like
a man who had spent his life hanging
     from I-beams
        fifty stories above
teeming streets. Street poet
     sucking the hot life
  from a half-spent Old Gold,
       squeezed
between stone fingers, lips pursing
     past a vague memory of incisors,
        satin jacket city-stained
picked from the discard pile at
          a mission on Avenue A.
     Two shoes looking
as though they'd followed Dean and Sal Paradise
    from Macdougal to The Golden Gate
on foot.   He drank with

Kerouac, for sure.
Knew him dead and alive. Survived
        on an over-sized liver and heart
to talk about
                the old days and days
before them. Now
        Burroughs is hawking NIKES on MTV,
Ginsberg sporting chainstore Khakis
                in The New Yorker to the
children of the X Generation who
wouldn't know a beat from a thud.
        Ya gotta do whutya can do to get by,
                he says between downbeats.
        Still he knows it's best to have a friend
with a spare plate and fork and
                a soft bed where,
in the dead of night
        you can hear the call of
a far off freight lumbering over
two cool rails to
                                Somewhere.

William Carlos Williams Gets a Haircut

At the salon, the ladies
of suburbs drift
in, drop in appointed
or not
From the malls or school-
yards or formica kitchens
clutching infants with
gold earrings or
parcel treasures.
Angie and Terri and
Nick's wife Josie.
The air is thick
with tart fragrance
and acetone and chit-
chat on the verge
of tears or slander.
They press rouged
cheeks and kiss
the air and say
Hiya, and My God, I
haven't seenya since
liddle Lisa's Chrissnin',
Howz Mikey and da kidz?
And they all reply Whatsa
use complaining'?
From your mouth to Godz earz!
The linoleum is rife
with the dead-
ends of hairdos and
fingernails, the
mirrored walls reflecting
infinity.
Two fat women sit beneath
dryers and try
to read lips glancing
at recipes and sex
surveys in rabbit-

eared Glamour mags.
Bobbi says what color
for the nailz this week?
How about Dangerous Red?
The lady in the satin sweats sits
wet headed in chair number three.
The tall redhead with silver
clips in her sleeves asks
Howdya like it Patti?
and she says just like
the lady in
number one
and number two
and four.
In chair number five
the poet says
Just a trim,
and
if you can,
add some on
top.

Some Call It Love
for Philip Appleman and Darwin

In truth it is only we humans who call it love
What the entirety of nature knows as propagation
the proud males displaying their immense maleness
driven beyond control by endocrine eruptions
to wild dances of courtship in the shadows
of deep green jungles and forests
and discotheques with ten dollar covers
Exploding arrays of manes and plumage
and pompadours glistening with perfumed lacquer
attempting under the over wound strain of
desperate Darwinian overdrive
to curry the attentions of the ever reluctant female
blue with the burden of unfailing discretion
handing out rejection and humiliation
like bittersweet penny confections
Pondering the insufferable battles
and certain conjugations to come
Coyly sipping drinks at the bar
adorned with paper umbrellas
He exploring her scent like a holiday meal
She wondering if he will make a good
first impression upon meeting the folks
Hoping he won't cast her aside after her labor's done
for some younger peacock or lioness
or blonde with yet firm breasts
For they all know that a man's got to do
what a man's got to do
Soaring over mountain tops roaming the jungle floor
Staying out in bowling alleys until after midnight
Drinking the glories of his manhood from
the screenplay of nature and a frosted mug
Dangling on sinewy strings of slime from musty limbs
Snapping gum in slow motions of
the mirror balled strobe lights
Begging the stares of the ever erect who come
to shuffle the linoleum caverns in

double knit gift wrap and Italian loafers
It's the way of the game
the royal piggyback minuet
The Black widow's mate gladly coming to death
Never surviving to tell tales of conquest
How she had begged him for even more
and the whimpering pleas left on his answering machine
Certain she won't respect him in the morning
Lying back exhaling great plumes of satisfaction
into the steamy air of candlelit rooms
Howling at the moonbeams dripping on the forest floor
Each creature awaiting the evolution of the headache
Stalking the bars for the two martini conquest
And a chance to find a piece of the happily ever after
Sailing the high seas aboard the Beagle with Darwin
On a journey through time to a couch in Vienna.

Inspiration

In the violescent
evenings I sit,
waiting
for the hum of
gyros and whirligigs
inside my egg-shell
skull, to resume my
living, to bring up
a fresh fount from
a dry place.

Some of my children
live on pages which,
on windless nights,
I rustle in my fingertips to
emulate the absent
breeze.
I say to them,
Listen hard,
for the footsteps
of the zephyr
are easy to miss
in this darkness
disconsolate.

God

He is the beginning and the end
The bearer of all forevers.
His finger tips swirl galaxies
His eye sees the very codes of life.
With his mercy he brought forth purgatory
and men with two cheeks.
In his wisdom he wished a deluge upon the earth
and fashioned Darwin from the muck.
He is more than we dare know and
yet less than we can imagine.
He made tinmen and popes, black holes
and the aurora borealis, nickels and himalayas.
He is love and love
is blind.
He loves a good fight.
He enjoys his fame.
He had me fail geometry and
made trees which became the masts of ships
and the bunks in death camps.
He conceived of hummingbirds and nuclear physics.
He is indeed most righteous.
In his firmament evil never triumphs.
He makes plaster madonnas weep and
causes deserts and cancer and snowflakes
and stillbirths and fireflies and widows
and shadows and the apocalypse.
He knows everyone by name and
He listens to prayers.
He is the landlord, the taxman
and the concierge.
He is surely one
of us.

Harlem Sunday Afternoon

Up here, the city has
not changed for fifty
years, only the deepened
blues hanging crepe
over the geometry of
tenement rows; the
percussive calling
of fears and anger
pounding ceaseless
against crumbling
brick.
On the corner of
Martin Luther King and
Malcolm X Blvds., at
the vortex of despair,
a most splendid lady, head
to toe in Sunday meeting
best: white wool, white
leather, white rabbit and
a grand white chapeau.
She was pride and jazz
and angel dignity, eyes
aloft, scaling the ruins
and invisible to
everyone but
the poets.

Atheists

We keep death
like an old
suit of clothes
we hang in the
guest room closet
at the far end
of the hallway.
Some days we
draw open the door,
remember it's
still there
preserved for us.
We smell the darkness,
one day find some
forgotten scrap
in some forgotten
pocket.
We withdraw
and close the door
for now.
We walk to an open
window for
reassurance and
find it
in a distant view.

A Love Story

She loved
Him
like moss loves
stone.

And

He loved
Her
like a whore loves
earrings.

When the kids' braces were
all paid up
He tossed
Her on the heap like
a bald tire.

And

She took
Her
tears and
left.

After Having Lost It

I imagine me
in the asylum
playing ping-pong
in someone else's
old robe and slippers.
The lissome ball arrives.
I return it.
It comes once more.
I do the same.
Nuthouse MUZAK
swirls at my feet,
floats into the earz
through the headz
of a roomful of men
souls who forgot why
to get up in the morning.
I remember,
but won't say anything
except
"My serve? .... or yours?"

With Ignatow At Whitman's Birthplace
13Nov94

With you here
on Paumonok where
the West Hills rise,
wrapped in
sacred cedar shake,
you sit framed
beneath a south-facing
twelve-over-eight
pane window which
gathers the mid-November
sun,

Granting you
a helm of light
before spilling
upon the floorboards
in this place where
Whitman drew
the first drops of nectar
from mother and moment.
In this home
we can sing out for
yesterday and tomorrow.

In this home
we can be children always.

In this home
you are the perfect
son.

News Report 31 January 91: Due to a lack of available space at National Cemeteries in the New York City area, casualties of Operation Desert Storm will be interred at Calverton National Cemetery on Long Island.

Calverton

In memory of Manuel Rivera, Jr.
first New York City casualty,
Operation Desert Storm

Lead me not in warrior's robes,
Like those knights and knaves of yore,
Nor through the dim to distant fields,
Where wretched battles rage and roar.
For I've not malice in my soul,
Despise not faceless foe I seek,
Nor bloodlust want of victory,
For those ones daring but to speak.

Cast not aside immortal youth,
As so much chaff upon the breeze,
Across the mead where devils dwell,
Against the ire of stormy seas.
This duty, as this night, grows stark,
Naught but dread keeps me from reason,
Sad circumstance, misfortune's spark,
Sure, no greater death than treason.

So lead me not to take my stand,
A nether hero in the sun,
And lead me not to find my peace,
Beneath the sod of Calverton.

After Keats Ode to a Nightingale

Prepare for me the feast divine,
A table so resplendent.
A place to sip the timeless wine,
From vineyards of contentment.
I dread not nightfall's mystery,
From this vantage in twilight,
As did I then a youthful me,
Swathed in morning dewlight,

Mine ear is cocked in deference,
To those far winds beckoning,
To let eternity commence,
My faithless mortal reckoning.
A nightingale at garden's gate,
Serenades this fractured hour,
Such strains to cause my soul elate,
Making rumbling darkness cower.

Forever, be this my final thought?
Eyes full with this perfection?
This raspy growl what time has wrought?
The furrowed face, this reflection?
Age, cruel as the driver's whip,
Sting of winter cross my back,
While fires of life fall from my grasp,
Pastel sunrise fades to black.

Shadow, spare not sad insistence,
Death knell, waste not salty tears.
Heart will cease without resistance,
When the day of darkness nears.
With age my gnarly fingers ache,
Expression eludes like a virgin.
Face burns now with each icy flake,
of snows silent but urgent.

So, mock me not you wistful youth,
Cast no fretful eye upon me,
But heed the word senescence speaks,
Too soon calling out to thee.

Pride

She is most proud
her
Sicilian Mother-in-Law
approves
of her sauce.

Her husband
gets
angry playing
solitaire
washing dishes

Complains
about her complaints.

Each night
she
brushes her hair
her teeth
scrubs away

The day from
her
face, it's
time for bed
soon time to

Awaken again.

Omar Geometrics
for Alan Shields

Gold earring dome
under mantra headdress
SPIDER S T R U N G
woodpulpsuperimpositions
Indian b e a d perennial
candycanes in greensandsnows
F E S T O O N I N G
B l a c k m a p l e space
with
microdonut-spectrums
S T R U N G   L I K E   G A R L A N D
across
Sky-conscious-middays
by
COSMOPRISMATIC OCCURRENCE.

Return to EARTH
Its own spherical perfection
Return to TREES
their
Cream-slurry hearts
C O N T E M P L A T E
kansas meatballs
beneath
fuzedquartz panels
THE WIREBEASTIES DANCE and
swing in
s c a l l o p s h a c k s h a d o w s
mute eloquence
TANGENTS AND CIRCUMLOCUTION
and
O M A R   G E O M E T R I C S

The Old Fireman's Home and Museum
Hudson, New York Oct. 94

The firemen built a home
of brick and mortar,
between two mountains,
where they could sit
in the shrinking sunlight.
Beside a sad smolder of embers
a museum filled with
old pumpers and scarred helmets,
commendations for courage.
Satin banners from the likes of
The Highland Hose Company
The Speigeltown Volunteers.
An eighteen-twelve Gooseneck
A twenty-six American LaFrance,
still shining with
the red-chrome brashness of youth.

On a great lawn, shade trees,
the autumn air hung like a black crepe
over an old man on a porchswing,
two on a quiet green bench.
Many more forsaken heros
sit and age in grace
beside open windows. All around
the dying of summer
has set the treetops and hills afire.
In this repose they listen
for the song of brass bells
and the call to the flames, but
they hear none, this October day.

An Ascension
for Jacqueline Bouvier

No one should die
In the Spring
Not when the trees
Are shimmering
In the green ascension
Nor when the finches
Are darting among
The branches calling out
To all who will listen
"See here, it is Spring and
We are alive!"

No one should leave us
In the Spring
But the white recall
of Winter
On days such as this
Reincarnate in
Color and Cantatas
We could lose everything
Everything
And still
Have

Hope.

Shelter Island Presbyterian Sunday

It was a razor perfect Sunday,
half past an Indian October eleven,
the weighty oak doors spread,
wide as the preacher's arms,
on the chaste white church,
the Presbyterians raised up
in a simpler day,
with a steeple true and
near to heaven as a ladder could reach.
Then out pour the faithful;
men in solitary suits;
angelic ladies on arm beneath
great hats felt and feathered.
Children suffering in
white linen and spitshined shoes,
imagining bluejeans and baseballs
and dollies home waiting.
While deep in their shadows,
The old graveyard sits silent
and collects falling leaves;
Knowing well it's only time
no God-fearing man can refuse;
Aware only the living can see
daylight dance through stained-glass.
The dead cannot green
when the Spring comes again;
They can but witness forever
from below the hard surface.

They say the leaves fall but once
in the season of man.

Water

The summer sun
sucks the moisture
from my zillion pores
up to heaven
I suppose

To be later used
to water lawns
and shade trees
feed oceans
and waterfalls

One drop at a time
trickling
down from my brow
and the
small of my back

Up to the clouds
for a trip
round the world,
parachuting
back down to Earth

Making the tiniest
splash
and
ripple
in a puddle in Peking.

B-Movie

When you were about
two
one evening
during your bath
I tossed you
some toys
to keep you
amused.
All at once, you
began screaming.
Not a terrible
two's scream, but
a convincing
B-Movie when
the beautiful blonde
encounters
the monster in her
closet or rear-
view mirror scream.
Your Mother
rushed in and in
a swoop
fetched the evil
from the soap-blue water
"He's afraid of
Barbies with no heads".
Yes, I thought, of course.

Safe Sex

Back
in the nineteen fifties
When Levittown
and Hulahoops
and The Ink Spots
were all
Front Page News,
My Mother
marched through
the first volleys
of the sexual revolution
with valor and dignity,
First reaching puberty
then dating
some guy named Cecil
then meeting
and marrying my Father.

The bride, of course
wore white.

Real Blonde

I had this dream you see
Black Ferrari top down
A mad redhead right beside me
Spring in our eyes
Hair bent against the wind
Like palm leaves in a typhoon
The whole world
Feeling the electricity
Of this April day
Nothing but blue above beyond
And nothing following
She wants me more
Than immortality and
My heart is pounding harder
Than a four-thirty Friday jackhammer

Then

The blonde wakes me suddenly
With a good kick to the shin
And tells me
I was snoring.

Testosterone

And so they emerged
from every home
The Huntsmen
bidding farewell
to mothers and babies
Laugh they did
in camouflage
and well-oiled boots
Off into
The Sacred Wilderness
to become one
with creation
to taste
the living air
drink of
the autumn sun
Painted Warriors
draped in the
shades of conquest
the ceremonial robes
of manhood
So they filled themselves
with tales of hunts past and
when their bellies
were full enough
of ale and anticipation
they thought
as if all at once

Let us go now
and kill something.

A Trip to the Zoo

Today
I imagined Hell
might be a place
cordoned
with rusty chickenwire
filled with
the very driest dust
the stench
of piss and shit
in the dead breeze
and life's
most miserable creatures
covered with flies
and indignity.

To Stan Laurel

I wanted my daughter
to know you, who
you really were, where
you were born and when,
how you found Ollie.

See, he had a
blonde little girl
like you
and a beautiful wife
who loved him
and a grassy yard
filled with friends.

Stan, it's sad
you can't know her.
She loves you
like vanilla icecream
with sprinkles,
a favorite uncle who
lives in a box
in the den.

You would love
to hear her when
she says to me
with such impatience,
"Can we watch Stan and Ollie, now?"

A Letter to Grandfather

The day your heart gave up, I
was spindly, blue-eyed,
two months shy
of twelve. When you
left, you left
a hole in living
the size of Croon's Lake.
Of all your slight possessions,
my Father chose a gold WALTHAM,
the one you bought yourself
to celebrate the joyous
depravity of retirement.
Fifteen years later it
was mine.
Ten years hence, it
no longer runs, still
I wear it faithfully,
my spare memory of you
mattering so much more
than the counting of time.

Eulogy

At the graveside of
his Father,
my Father
stands upon
the quivering
January earth.
The razorwind
slashes at all of us,
huddled against
the cold loss
and death.

From a scrap
of paper he reads
and it snaps
in his fingers.
His voice breaks
as the words of it
rise upon from
within him.

The lives of flowers are too brief.

Every young boy
should see
his Father
weeping his
broken heart
into his hands,
at least once.

It's only death
can make us men,
after all.

Shelter Island August

This day
feels as though
it will never rain
again
the deepness of
the azure sky
blemished only
by the
occasional
cottonwool marauder
or
flash of feather.

But see
the pond is
dry
the earth is
terracotta
and
all that's still
green
beneath
the ever
saffron sun
tires and grows more ashen.

The Nature of Forgiveness

The counterman at
the Lexington Ave. Deli
doesn't care
about my cholesterol
or about
what I think.
He concerns himself
with just two things:
whether my
corned beef on rye
is just one quarter inch
taller than
the height of my
jaws fully opened
and
whether I want
a pickle.
(If not, I assume
he will save it
for someone who does.)

But I want him
to step back
from his counter
a moment, remove
the stubcigar from
his bitter lips,
ask me if
I am satisfied
with my life,
if I sleep well
at night, if
someone loves me.
But he has
no time to spare.
With one stroke
he cleaves me in two
and hands me the bag
without a word.

I decide to forgive him.

Do Spacemen Pass Dead Souls On Their Way To the Moon?

Do spacemen pass
dead souls
on their way to
the moon?
Whispers with faces,
floating through
the empty heavens
like cumulus elegies,
searching
for the valley where
Elysium lies?

From two hundred
thousand miles
up, the world
is smooth and blue
and dipped
like a candy apple
in serenity.

The moon
calls it
Eden.

Shipwrecks

Living beneath
the cusp of whitecaps
Surfaces sparkle like
dimestore charms.
I look beneath
and wonder deep
at depth.
Seabound I contemplate
Jupiter's moons
beyond reach of
outstretched arms.
All horizons fold
under the cape
of the sky.
At the apex of night
they become one
with black and stars
with living oceans and shores
with all soft notions
of infinity.

For Yo-Yo Ma

It was not long ago,
That your bones ached
beneath your young fingertips.
Other children's voices
danced with whim and wildflowers
in all the places, you
had abandoned for the sake
of destiny.

Now your quiet passions
pour like cream
from a silver ewer,
Your face bearing the colors
of every human moment,
Your sonance an embrace.
You say listen to
these things I do

With a few strands
of gut and wire.

Finding Jesus

My wife, Victoria
found Jesus
on a beach
Saturday past.
Well, actually just
his head.
Not his real
head, of course
but a small
silver one
on a chain.
Maybe not silver.
In any case,
now he's been
saved, and
he sits on the
kitchen counter
looking into
the fluorescence,
while his savior
puts up a pot
for tea.

The Nature of Worship

It's what you wanted
all along, someone
to aim your eyes
skyward, giving
names to each star,
as if they might
answer when you
call out to them.
Still, you must know
that the night
is only a hole
with no bottom.
The constellations
of the Romans and Greeks
survive countless lives,
yet are not
eternal.

You believe that
sleep is the antidote for longing.

For me,
there is no comfort
in darkness.
Each night
the last face I see
is mortality.
My last thought:
a reason to awaken again.
My prayers for one thing:
that tomorrow
one more green sapling will
rise up and flower; that
I might be there to see it.

A Broken Line in the Snow

I am sitting alone in
this amber room.
I am thinking of you.
Outside, a December wind
scatters this morning's snow
across an icy crust,
like glass dust.
Even water can be
lifeless at times such
as these, empty of
all but the memory
of flowing, of dripping
without effort down
from petals and rooftops.
In the new mantle
of snow, the deer
have left the friable
marks of their journey.
To them April is but
abstraction, yet they
continue on, never knowing
if winter will cease,
if they will ever again
see the mist embrace
the meadow at daybreak.
They told you
the tumor was big as a
tennis ball, a black hole
into which your
life was falling, safe
within the nest
of your flesh and bone,
a comrade to the dark,
A broken line
in the snow.

There Are the Long Days

There are the long days
When I can
Only look toward sleep
To close my heavy eyes
Turn off the cinema
That daylight pours
Through my windows.

Outside it's only
The crickets who refuse
To honor the shrouded
Silence.
In a distant room
The television speaks
To the furniture,
My children practice abandon.

There are the long days
When I consider
Gouging out my eyes
With all of these
Spiked expectations.
That I might spend
All of the long days
Needing only
To find a way through
The Dark.

Melancholy

You don't get skies
much bluer
than this one.
Incandescent.
A lamp globe lit
in a darkened room.

See how

Nothing dares
to move, to upset
the perfection.
The way it is
with deep, lovely
blueness.

The way

It can
draw the world
In, and
not let go.
Maybe
Never let go.

The Nature of Love

In Mrs. Clark's
First Grade class
the first sentence
you ever scratched
was

"I Love You"

In your life
it is a sentence
you will remember
and forget
and
hold like a
tiny bird in
your palm
Nearly crushing it
perhaps
ten thousand times.

For Happiness

Accept living
as a
well staggered
procession of
disappointments
with hope
the occasional
passing headlights
bursting through
the fence picket
casting
in a moment a
rolling black
and white cinema
on the wall:
Hope Despair Hope Despair Hope.

For Mary Oliver

In this drought,
living
I have carried
my goblet of
fallow earth,
trying long to
fill it with
just fog and dew.
In your forest
everything is

green and space.
From a ledge
high as
imagination
a waterfall
careens over
polished rock,
taking ease
in a pool of
tranquil sky, where

I bend
over blue and seek
reflection,
heart-broken
over a woman
I have never met.

Abraham and Son

Abraham was no spring chicken,
and having just barely survived
his son, Isaac's teen years,
not to mention God Almighty's edict
that he single-handedly populate Canaan.
He felt every day of his one hundred twenty years.
He did believe that there was beauty
in all of The Lord's creatures, but
the sight of his wife Sarah's
five score and six year old nakedness
rattled the foundations of his faith.
Still . . . ,
when God called out, "Abraham!"
his only reply was, "Here I am Lord."
Even when God ordered that he
change his name from "Abram" to
"Abraham", he thought to himself,
Could not the God of Ages, in his
wisdom come up with a better suffix
than "HAM". Oh!, the ribbing he took at Yeshiva!
Then there was that circumcision he
just had to have at age ninety-nine!
The pain!
And his cousin Lot, drunk as usual,
performing the delicate procedure,
shaky-handed and all. Then,
having to tell the tribes that
this was mandatory. Why,
even the thought of it gave him chicken-flesh.
But this, this was going too far.
Sure Isaac was never quite right after
his blind old Mother backed the family
cart over him, but
even Noah, old obsequious to a fault Noah,
even he could not barbecue his own son!
Imagine, The Almighty showing up
unannounced at breakfast this morning,
saying with a straight face to
"Offer him as an holocaust upon
one of the mountains I will shew thee."
And Abraham was certain it was The Lord
because he knew how The Lord
loved his Ed Sullivan and also
that he was the only one who would say,

"an holocaust".
He protested bitterly under his breath
and continued gathering wood.
What, for the love of Mike, could he do?
He had seen God smite entire cities for
lesser offenses than simple disobedience and
after all, he still had hundreds of
other children and —
Isaac was kind of a dimwit.
So . . . . ,
he did the only reasonable thing and
grabbed Isaac by the ear and
headed for the mountains.
After three days, they finally reached
the place of The Lord (which was nothing
to write home about) and found the altar
The Lord had prepared.
Abraham was itching to get back
So . . . . . ,
He hog-tied the boy faster than
Tom Mix on diet pills and
tossed him on the heap.
Isaac was growing concerned
then just as Abraham raised his sword
above his head and prepared
to skewer the lad,
The angel of The Lord appeared and said,
"Chill thou out!"
And Abraham did chill, just in the nick of time.
And while Isaac was getting out of
his wet loincloths,
God from the heavens popped out his head saying,
"Abraham, you give me great joy, that
thou wouldst sacrifice thy son for me.
Because you are such a mensch, I will
multiply your seed like the stars of heaven
and the sand that is by the seashore."
This is not what Abraham wanted to hear.
Sarah was pushing a hundred and twenty.
He was thinking a little timeout in
the desert would be a good idea
Then,
the Lord said, "Sin to waste that fire,
go grab that lamb."
And they ate like kings and gave
thanks to The Lord for remembering
the mint Jelly.

Gestation
for James Genovese

Days and months
pass like years
and more years
You swell with
another life
feeling as though
You are being
devoured from
the inside
one gram one vowel
at a time.

Near the end

You can only sit
and add the sunsets
Like a trainman
You put the minutes
into Your pocket
When the certain
day arrives
You heave and gasp
turn your insides out
to the waiting crowd
And when

The houselights
come up again
You find that
Your baby is gone
and
gone for good.

The Nature of Mortality

Your worried look becomes
a question.
"Am I going to die,
someday?"
I offer you
my most gentle,
"yes",
But I say,
"Not for a very
long time. Not until
you are very
very very VERY old."
"How old?",
you say.
"One hundred."
I reply.
"How old was
Greatgrandma
when she died?"

"eighty five."

"How much is that
away from
one hundred?"

Realizing now
that I have been cornered
by innocence and
metaphysics, I say,
"Why are you even worrying
about such things?
Afterall, I've only yesterday
taken the training wheels
off of your bicycle."

The Nature of Respect

The gulls
must be starving.
Everything, everywhere
is frozen solid.
Birds are left
only sky.
I throw crumbs
onto the new snow.
First the bluejays,
then a lone flicker,
then the gulls.

They swoop down
in whitegray overcoats,
standing erect
in new shoes and
gangster shoulders,
hair straight back
and perfect.
Aiming their
fedoras
into the unforgiving
wind, they
take what they want.

Left to the trees
even the crows are
angry and bitter,
wishing to be
many miles from
the sea.

The Man On a Leash

Along side the Korean
Grocer, a brown
pit-bull with a young
urban wise-ass on
his leash, stopped at
the blue dumpster so
that the wise-ass could
relieve himself.
The pit-bull gazed
about the scene
nervously; partly for
caution and partly for
nonchalance.

The wise-ass having
immodestly completed
his business, shook-back
and turned.
"What can I tell you, I
had to go."
The pit-bull said
nothing but continued
to look menacing.
The light changed and
the grocer realigned his
apples one
more time.

The Nature of Virtue

My children
do not know
that winter
is just beyond
the maple empyrean,
across
the shimmering bay.
In the dormant
grass they run
and chase one another
and shout their
wild thoughts
up at the drape
of Autumn.

To them
joy is
the sunshine
over a soft shower
of painted leaves
on some meadow
of childhood.
I watch them
from a small distance
and I draw in
a crisp breath
of memory
and
let it pour out
slowly.

Austerlitz, New York—Autumn 1993
for Edna St. Vincent Millay

There is a storm
crawling up the back
of the peaked fresco,
billowing victorious
from warring with sunset.
The oaks on the ridge quiver.
Windchime at meadow's gate
hands three notes
to the wind.
There a finch
told me that
the lady of
Steepletop gathered
songbirds and sky
and hillside and blossom
and gave each a
page in the book
of sonnets.
The finch was
sure it was true.

The crickets had
told him so.

Beatitude for Uris

Blessed are they
who hear the tones
of truth and history,

Pleading in
arcane murmurs
from the darkness,

And are waiting
nearby with lantern
and wonder.

For Pablo Neruda

My eyes do not see
what is ahead or
behind, but only
beyond.

There are trains in
my head which
ramble without ceasing.
Percussive
miles of boxcars,
some empty, some
full and bolted tight.

The landscape
is ever-changing,
the trainman's face
never visible.
People and moments
board and
disembark, station
to station.

Through night
and mountains,
the wind that follows
everywhere is also

loneliness.

Massapequa

I was, as I recall, a child once
in this great suburban garden of eden
called Massapequa
named with the executioner's reverence
for a small tribe of Indians
who had disappeared from the face of the Earth
leaving little more than a name
and a meager handful of arrowheads
now displayed proudly in a case at the library.
It seems time began with the second world war
which left millions dead and even more
on the GI Bill
with their heads full of visions
of sixty by one hundred and electric every
damned things and big fat Fords full of
kids and dogs named Prince and cheap gasoline
It was from these humble seeds that sprung
the true Massapequans
who grew up wanting to be commuters
and telling the folks back in St. Albans
and Red Hook and on 123rd Street in Harlem
about lawn mowers and tiny beds of Burpee marigolds
and trees which grew honest to goodness apples
which looked good enough to eat though they weren't.
It was the Life Magazine American Dream
die cast stainless steel red brick stoop
if you can't get it in Sears it ain't worth having.
And I wasn't alone back in 1962
showing up in Massapequa while Jack Kennedy
was still the fearless ivory smile leader
of the legions of leisure.
We sang the uplifting strains of
America the Beautiful in thirty-two part harmony
every morning at eight thirty sharp
and we studied it all to secure our own
little square in the bright and polished
chrome plated future.
We walked the streets with bats and balls and
Micky Mantle signature mits

tried hard to kneel up straight through
Mass every Sunday at eleven
dressed in blue blazers and starched cotton
like miniature Dashing Dans and Annette Funicellos
right off the racks of Mays across the tracks
where Massapequan mothers waited in
Country Squire wagons with Detroit wood on the side
for the gates to fall for the 4:59
out of Penn Station
It was like a movie set on a backlot in heaven
Beautiful homes lining the streets named
for fruit trees and Presidents
like pieces on a Monopoly board
cars in driveways proud with last Saturday's wax
and lawns cut and trimmed like felt patches
and kids, more kids than anyone thought conceivable
filling the streets and yards and the corner
candy store with many things for a penny
and egg creams in tall glasses for two bits
all full of the most glorious chatter and churning
until dusk when every home was lit with
the iridescent glow of Walter Cronkite
and Lucy and Desi before syndication
and we were sure there was no sorrow and that
all our secrets were little ones and
we were all looking up to people named
Ozzie and Ward and Bishop Sheen
and we all spent our days admiring the sky
and the smell of cut grass and the news
that Mrs. So and so down near the corner
of Buchanan and North Walnut Street was expecting again
that no one ever noticed the bars
and the grass in bureau drawers
and that the richest man in town
was the one who built fences

The seven daughters of Atlas, the Pleiades, grieving over his death, were transformed by Zeus himself into doves which he sent into the heavens to join the constellation of Taurus. The seventh Pleiade later became invisible to the naked eye and has ever since been referred to as The Lost Pleaide.

The Lost Pleiade

There is the moment
Just as the most humble
Autumn sun lays its
Crimson mantelet over
The graying shoulders
Of the evening,
Just as the transcendent
Notes of the nightingale
Become hushed by slumber
The cicadas and crickets
Call out to crescendo.
Between the soft-pebbled
Stream and a rock
Even the gods could not
raise up from the Earth,
It will rain just enough;
Make forest glisten with greens
Festooned in spiderwebs
Hung like silver filament
Strung with diamond drips
The voices of silence
Chanting their certain joy
Into the treetop canopy.
Since days ancient meteor
She floats Earthward
Into the palmprint of Atlas
With sky gathered
Beneath her wings
In versicolor diadem
Making perfect Love
To the wind and milklight.
Touching, hovering
Over cool stillness

For but a moment
Grasping the hand of
The one adorned
Lifting her on opaline wing
Beyond frosted summits
Piercing dark distances
Above hope and up
Beyond any imagined wonder
Returning in time for
Wings to evanesce into
The Lavender eyes of dawn.
Daughter of Atlas
Lost from Zeus's perfect
Cluster of Doves
The seventh sister of Pleiades.

A Love Poem For Anyone Listening

In a square room split
By rapiers of light
Beneath the spider's diaphanous vortex
The tales of wicker
summers effervesce.
Through stenciled linen
The single note lingers
In search of consonance
The silent wishes of
Faeries and mourning doves.

Tell me something
That could not be true
In ten lifetimes

Tear me a rainbow
Into a memory of snow
Give me

The one thing
You would never let go
And my soul

Will be yours
Forever and always.

Sacraments

Seven,
in my first
blue suit,
on my knees
before
a tall man
draped to
a marble floor
in saint satins.
From his
golden plate
my first taste
of flesh.
From his
golden goblet
my first taste
of blood.

My parents
smiled and cried.

Back home
carloads of relations
around a
well-stocked bar
admired the smell
of charcoal smoke
and a sheet-cake
of chocolate
and buttercream
adorned with
the cross of Jesus.
In the envelopes
enough loot
for a sting-ray bike
and those shoes
I was needing.

Later on
The bike was stolen.
I outgrew the shoes.
I became a vegetarian.

Of Horses, Woodpeckers, Starships and Supermen

What world is this
    where
darkness can never be
      too bright
   nor
might too subtle;
where no man
    no machine
can be
     too soft
too certain.

In this life
    we must ever
   consider   the unthinkable
    so to
marvel at   respect
   the least of the living
    who can halt
both
    Spaceships and Supermen
with only
   a sharp beak   and
    a hesitation

What Charles Simic Made Me Wonder
16July95

Before

                alarm clocks

did people still

        awaken?

    When

phones

                      ring

        we

    answer

        never knowing

if

    the news

   will be

       good.

I wonder

    who

      do we thank

 for

   the sorrows

        we can now

    aim

through   the   atmosphere

    like darts

  sailing   upon

      the

   brightly colored

      f e a t h e r s

    of

  dead birds?

Ritual

Empty-headed
winter day

sitting

before an
oakfire hearth

tossing

failures
one by one

flaming

lights consume
stillborn inspirations

casting

the dust
of them

upward

to a
focus of

sky.

A Hard Day's Nightmare

Imagine
my horror
walking
into the
steamy loo
only to
find you
in the shower
with Ringo
himself
your hands
full of suds
playing
in his
Octopus's Garden.

You know
they could hear
the echo
of my heart
shattering
on the tile
all the way
to the
docks of
Liverpool.
At least
it
was
not
Paul.

The Man Making Fortune Cookies

In this dim-lit factory
along the broad Chang
where the sweet-air
is hung heavy with the
purple plums of wisdom,
a graying man stands
in The Peoples' Blues
and hand-made sandals,
typing out in red letters,
the futures of us all.
And with ancient ingenuity
weaves them through a
slight curl of confection,
which must also
give up its life
in the end.
In his head
the words of Chuang-tzu
folding over and over
and today like every day
he knows not whether
he is a man
dreaming he is a butterfly
or a butterfly
dreaming he is a man.

Peter Pan's Elegy
for Jerry Garcia

Because
He
Could
Fly,
We
Thought
He
Would
Live
For
Ever.

Twentieth Reunion—Alfred G. Berner High

28July95

The first woman
I ever loved was
sixteen and lovely
and didn't love me.
Three days in June,
my back blistering
beneath the stares
of an unforgiving sun,
I slagged whitewash
over your grandfather's dock
for enough money
to see us to the prom.

That night
after we danced
in our platform shoes
beneath innocence
and handpainted stars,
you left my dream
and fell into the arms
of the basketball hero.
I can tell you now,
I sobbed walking home
without you
blue suit and eyes,

Invisible in the darkness.
This night it's you
who might cry
thinking of all the poems
you never heard.

Those Crazy Seventies

Remember that one,
When Mrs. Brady was away
in some distant and Unknown Burg,
And Alice slipped on the Chinese Checkers
(and all those colored marbles)
and sprained her right ankle
(thank goodness it wasn't broken)
And the Doc said she had to stay off it
And Mr. Brady and the kids had to pitch-in
And Alice almost missed the Meat-Cutters Ball
But then Mrs. Brady got home
(just in the nick of time)
And relieved the bedlam
And Alice danced on her crutches
and her one good foot
And finally got a goodnight kiss
from her date, the butcher.
The next week
everything was back to normal.
How did they do it?

The Poet is Out

Sorry
that
I am
not here
to
greet you.

You see
the moon
is new
and
I am
out in

the darkness
hunting
fireflies.
Please
leave
a message.

What Happened One Day On Midway Road

Passing Gracie's
I had to
swerve widely
to avoid
a head-on
with Jimmy Gibbs
coming on
around
some guys
from the
highway crew
fixing a hole
causing me
to almost
run down
one of
Anderson's geese.
Jimmy Gibbs
waved as he passed
the bigger goose
honked out
something
I won't repeat
and the
highway guys
never noticed.

By the time I got home
they had all turned
into this poem.

Morning On West Neck Bay

A bayman
rises alone
upon the
satin of an
early April dawn
balancing a
flatwood bottom
beneath
unsoiled boots
over the first
suggestion of
reflected sky.

Wire-mesh
upon a
man-length pole
he resurrects
immortal
blackmud and
takes as gift
whatever is offered
to his tired hands
and the arms
of the
rising Spring light.

All I Know About Dorothy Parker

Dorothy Parker lived
beneath grand hats
that would cast
sorrowful shadows
upon the
slope of her cheek,
her eyes playing
to her smoke like
the cobra charmer's songs.
Day and night
she spent inhabiting
windowless rooms
inside her head.
Tasting the lying lips
of her bottleneck lover,
her tongue hurled spears
through both granite
and flesh and
although she wore her sadness
like a wet wool cape,
They would always
ask her, Dorothy,
say something
to make us all
laugh.

War Games

The two of us
assembled armaments
and armies
stood them
face to face
across an expanse
of tongue and groove
prepared ourselves
for the
coming carnage.
His Storm Troopers for The Fatherland
My Marines for all that is good.
My artillery fired first.
I fell struck on the forehead
by his biggest aircraft carrier
He went off to bed
with no kiss goodnight

and then

There was peace once more.

Collector's Item

This poem
is being
issued in an
as yet
undetermined
number.
With a
cryptic
signature
it is nothing
if not
decorative
especially in
a tasteful
frame.
Sometime
after you and I
are long dead
one of
your descendants
will try
to sell it off.
I can
only hope
they do.